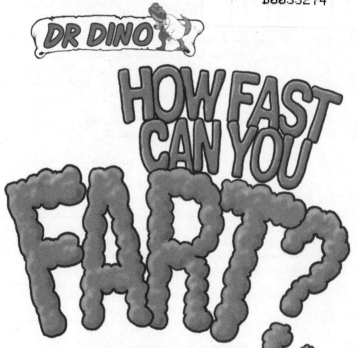

Dr Dino's Learnatorium

DINO

Published by Dino Books,
an imprint of John Blake Publishing Ltd,
3 Bramber Court, 2 Bramber Road,
London W14 9PB, England

www.johnblakepublishing.co.uk

www.facebook.com/Johnblakepub 🖪
twitter.com/johnblakepub 🖪

First published in paperback in 2014

ISBN: 978-1-78219-766-9

British Library Cataloguing-in-Publication Data:

A catalogue record for this book is available from the British Library.

Design by www.envydesign.co.uk

Printed in Great Britain by CPI Group (UK) Ltd

3 5 7 9 10 8 6 4 2

Papers used by John Blake Publishing are natural, recyclable products made
from wood grown in sustainable forests. The manufacturing processes conform
to the environmental regulations of the country of origin.

Every attempt has been made to contact the relevant copyright-holders,
but some were unobtainable. We would be grateful if the appropriate
people could contact us.

Introduction

School is important, but you can't learn everything there. In fact, you can't learn nearly everything. The only place you can do that is in my wonderful learnatorium. Your teachers will tell you the boring stuff like how to divide 1200 by 5, who Henry VIII's six wives were or how to use a full stop and a comma, but there's a whole world of bizarre facts and unbelievable information out there that they won't bother with. For example:

Do you know who the most unlucky football fan in the world is?

Do you know what colour carrots used to be?

Do you have any idea what hippopotomonstroses-quippedaliophobia means?

Do you know which dinosaurs are still around today (except for me, of course. I'm a pretty special case)?

Do you know how many senses humans actually have (hint: it's not five)?

If the answer to all of these is yes, then there's probably no point in reading any further. Congratulations! You know everything! But if the answer is no then this book is the one for you. It's packed with important facts from my learnatorium that you really need to know. I can teach you about everything from your own body to the deepest reaches of space to the smallest particles in the Universe. And at the end of the book you will even find a little quiz to test just how much you've learned. So sit back, put your reading glasses on (that's if you're one of the estimated 65% of people who need them) and get reading!

Dr Dino

A Little Bit About You
to Start Off With

Your thumb is the same length as your nose.

It takes food just seven seconds to travel from your mouth to your stomach.

On average you (and every other person) fart about once an hour. That's 8,760 farts every year, which adds up to 700,800 farts in your lifetime. Phew, that's a lot of gas!

Human thigh bones are stronger than concrete. I wouldn't recommend kicking a concrete wall though...

It doesn't matter what day you were born on, you share a birthday with at least 10,000,000 other people in the world.

It is impossible to sneeze with your eyes open. What's more, a sneeze travels out of your mouth at a whopping 100 miles per hour! No wonder you can't keep it in.

Dr Dino's Did You Know?

People first started saying 'God Bless You' back in the Middle Ages. This was because in those days even the smallest illness could end up in death, so the sound of someone sneezing was pretty scary. To try to protect the sneezer (and themselves!) from anything too serious people would bless them, something we still do today.

Food Colouring

The next time your parents serve up some unwanted carrots, tell them you only like the purple kind. Before the 16th century, almost all carrots were purple, but then in Holland some farmers grew mutant orange carrots in honour of the Dutch Royal Family – The House of Orange. You can still get purple carrots, but they're pretty rare.

Dr Dino's Trick For a Tan

If you eat enough carrots (and it has to be a lot) it's possible to turn your skin orange!

Carrots aren't the only food whose colour might have you fooled. Butter is naturally white – the yellow colour is artificial.

Not all colouring is artificial. Turnips turn green when sunburned.

Dr Dino's Did You Know?

There is no such thing as blue food. Even blue-berries are purple.

What's in a Name?

If you think where you live is crazy, think again. There is a town in West Virginia, USA, called Looneyville.

Probably the worst place to live is in Boring, in Oregon, USA. Just to make things worse, in 2002 Boring twinned with the village of Dull in Scotland.

The smelliest place to live has to be Middelfart, a town in Denmark.

With a whopping 85 letters Taumatawhakatangihanga-koauauotamateaturipukakapikimaungahoronukupokai-whenuakitanatahu is the longest place name in the world. It is a small hill in New Zealand, and it means 'The summit where Tamatea, the man with the big knees, the climber of mountains, the land-swallower who travelled about, played his nose flute to his loved one.' Try saying that in one breath!

Dr Dino's Did You Know?

Argentina's name means 'Land of Silver'. Stupidly, there is actually very little silver there.

Simon Bolivar was a great military leader in South America in the 19th century. He gave Colombia its name in 1819 and in 1825 Bolivia was named after him. Unfortunately, Bolivar was actually Venezuelan…

Ye Olde English

The oldest word in the English language is 'who'.

If your teacher ever tells you that you are using commas and full stops incorrectly, just tell them punctuation didn't even exist in writing until the 15th century, and people seemed to get on fine then!

Dr Dino's Did You Know?

People used to say 'ahoy-hoy' instead of 'hello' when answering the phone! In *The Simpsons* Montgomery Burns still answers the phone that way.

Shakespeare was a great inventor. In fact, he invented over 1,700 words in his plays, most of which we still use today such as champion, lonely, torture, bloodstained and swagger.

You might think the English language is fairly fixed by today, but you couldn't be more wrong. In fact, around 4,000 new words are created every year. By the time you are 20, there will have been more new words created in the English language (80,000) than the average person knows (75,000).

The Sizzling Sun

The Sun might look like it's the same size as the Moon, but this is just because it is so much further away. In reality you could fit 73,000,000 Moons inside the Sun.

The Sun is so far away it takes 8 minutes and 20 seconds for light from the Sun to reach the Earth. You might think that's not very long, but light travels at 299,792,458 metres per second! To think about that another way, if you were in a car that was going 90 miles per hour it would take you 118 years to get to the Sun. I hope you have some good car games to play!

Dr Dino's Did You Know?

The Sun releases so much energy that if a single drop from the core of the Sun was placed on the surface of the Earth, it would kill everything within 100 miles of that drop. That's what I call serious sunburn!

Because gravity is so much stronger on the Sun, a human weighing 60 kilograms on the Earth will weigh 1624 kilograms on the Sun. Incidentally, a dinosaur weighing 60 kilograms on the Earth will also weigh 1624 kilograms on the Sun.

Ridiculous Records

The world record for carrying a milk bottle on your head is 80.95 miles.

A Flemish artist painted the world's smallest hand-painted painting – a picture of a miller and his mill – on a single grain of corn. Scientists have also been able to recreate the *Mona Lisa* perfectly using machinery... at a third of the width of a human hair!

Dr Dino's Favourite Record

Michael Lotito holds the world record for the biggest airplane ever eaten. He also holds the world record for the only airplane ever eaten! He was born with stomach lining twice as thick as a normal person and could eat just about anything. It took him two years to chew his way through an entire Cessna plane.

The longest Monopoly game ever played lasted 70 days. However, in Buffalo, USA, someone decided playing normal Monopoly was a little too easy, and set up an underwater Monopoly tournament. To date the longest underwater game lasted 45 days.

In 2009 Jackie Bibby held 11 rattlesnakes in his mouth by their tails for 10 seconds, claiming one of the world's most dangerous world records.

Dr Dino's Did You Know?

Ashrita Furman holds the world record for... holding the most world records! As well as being the person who went 80 miles with a milk bottle on his head, he also holds records for things such as longest time balancing on a balance board (1 hour 49 minutes and 5 seconds), most garlic cloves eaten in 1 minute (22) and the furthest distance a water balloon can be thrown and caught without breaking (97 feet and 8 inches). Altogether he has achieved well over 200 world records!

Laws to
Die For

It is illegal for an MP to enter the House of Commons wearing a full suit of armour. Not only that, it is also against the law to die in the House of Commons. I don't quite know what the punishment would be...

In Scotland, you cannot be drunk and be in charge of a cow or a horse.

Dr Dino's Did You Know?

In 1998 it was made illegal to cause a nuclear explosion. Before then I assume it was only frowned upon by the police.

Be careful the next time you are sending a letter. It is an act of treason to place a postage stamp bearing the British monarch upside down on an envelope.

If you're Scottish, the best bet is to stay out of York. It is legal to kill a Scotsman within the city walls, but only if he is carrying a bow and arrow.

Weird Weather

You might think of the Sahara Desert as being pretty hot, but it has been known to snow there!

The windiest place on the planet is Common-wealth Bay, Antarctica where winds regularly top 150 miles per hour.

Dr Dino's Did You Know?

The wettest place in the world is Mawsynram in India, which gets 467 inches of rain a year on average. Mount Rainier in the USA is technically rainier... it holds the record for the most precipitation in one year – only it isn't for rainfall, but snowfall. In one year a whopping 1,225 inches of snow fell there!

Lightning strikes the Earth about 6,000 times per minute. And, contrary to what your teachers will tell you, it often strikes the same place twice.

The heaviest hailstones to ever fall to Earth weighed more than one kilogram each, and fell in a storm in Bangladesh. They caused enormous damage.

Dr Dino's Did You Know?

In the Middle Ages, church bells were rung and cannons fired to try to prevent hail from falling and damaging the crops. Now a slightly more successful technique called 'cloud seeding' is used, where planes are sent up to spray chemicals at the clouds. China did this with planes and rockets in 2008 during the opening and closing ceremonies at the Olympics to make sure that it didn't rain. Nobody asked why they didn't simply build a roof...

What Sort of a Word is That?

The longest published word in the English language is 1913 letters long and refers to a part of DNA. It is an enzyme that has 267 amino acids:

methionylglutaminylarginyltyrosylglutamylserylleucyl-
phenylalanylalanylglutaminylleucyllysylglutamylarginyl-
lysylglutamylglycylalanylphenylalanylvalylprolylphenyl-
alanylvalylthreonylleucylglycylaspartylprolylglycyliso-
leucylglutamylglutaminylserylleucyllysylisoleucylaspar-
tylthreonylleucylisoleucylglutamylalanylglycylalanylas-
partylalanylleucylglutamylleucylglycylisoleucylprolyl-
phenylalanylserylaspartylprolylleucylalanylaspartylgly-
cylprolylthreonylisoleucylglutaminylasparaginylalanyl-
threonylleucylarginylalanylphenylalanylalanylalanylgly-
cylvalylthreonylprolylalanylglutaminylcysteinylphenyl-
alanylglutamylmethionylleucylalanylleucylisoleucylargi-
nylglutaminyllysylhistidylprolylthreonylisoleucylprolyli-
soleucylglycylleucylleucylmethionyltyrosylalanylasp-
araginylleucylvalylphenylalanylasparaginyllysylglycyli-

soleucylaspartylglutamylphenylalanyltyrosylalanylgluta-
minylcysteinylglutamyllysylvalylglycylvalylaspartylseryl-
valylleucylvalylalanylaspartylvalylprolylvalylglutaminyl-
glutamylserylalanylprolylphenylalanylarginylglutami-
nylalanylalanylleucylarginylhistidylasparaginylvalylala-
nylprolylisoleucylphenylalanylisoleucylcysteinylprolyl-
prolylaspartylalanylaspartylaspartylaspartylleucylleucy-
larginylglutaminylisoleucylalanylseryltyrosylglycylargi-
nylglycyltyrosylthreonyltyrosylleucylleucylserylarginyl-
alanylglycylvalylthreonylglycylalanylglutamylasparaginy-
larginylalanylalanylleucylprolylleucylasparaginylhistidyl-
leucylvalylalanyllysylleucyllysylglutamyltyrosylasparagi-
nylalanylalanylprolylprolylleucylglutaminylglycylphenyl-
alanylglycylisoleucylserylalanylprolylaspartylglutaminyl-
valyllysylalanylalanylisoleucylaspartylalanylglycylala-
nylalanylglycylalanylisoleucylserylglycylserylalanyliso-
leucylvalyllysylisoleucylisoleucylglutamylglutaminylhis-
tidylasparaginylisoleucylglutamylprolylglutamyllysylme-
thionylleucylalanylalanylleucyllysylvalylphenylalanyl-
valylglutaminylprolylmethionyllysylalanylalanylthreonyl-
arginylserine

Rhythm and syzygy are the longest English words without vowels.

When two words are joined together to form a new word (breakfast + lunch = brunch) it is called a portmanteau.

Dr Dino's Did You Know?

It is often said that purple, orange, silver and month are the only words in English that don't rhyme with anything. However that is wrong. They rhyme with:

Purple – curple (a horse's bum), hirple (what it's called when you walk with a limp) and nurple (the act of twisting someone's nipple);

Orange – sporange (part of a mushroom) and Borenge (a hill in Wales);

Silver – chilver (a baby female lamb);

Month – Grunth (a sacred Hindu scripture).

The Eskimo language has over 100 words to describe different types of snow.

It's true that women speak more than men, almost three times as much in fact. The average woman speaks about 20,000 words a day. The average man speaks only about 7,000. This is only the case for humans though. In my experience male dinosaurs speak far more than female ones, but that might be because I'm the only one left...

Famous Last Words

Some people know just the right thing to say at the right time, and none more so than these men whose last words have gone down in history:

'My wallpaper and I are fighting a duel to the death. One or the other of us has to go.' – Playwright Oscar Wilde. The wallpaper stayed.

'Now, now, my good man, this is no time for making enemies.' – French philosopher Voltaire, after being asked to reject Satan.

Dr Dino's Did You Know?

One of my great heroes Albert Einstein, whose learnatorium was almost as big as mine is, could well have uttered the most extraordinary words on his deathbed... but we'll never know. He started speaking in German, but nobody there at the time could understand him!

'I want to die peacefully in my sleep like my grandfather. Not screaming in terror like his passengers.' – Jim Harkins.

'They couldn't hit an elephant at this dist...' – General John Sedgwick, who unfortunately miscalculated the distance the Confederate soldiers were away from him in the American Civil War.

'Don't let it end like this! Tell them I said something!' – Mexican revolutionary Pancho Villa, who couldn't think of anything to say.

The Marvellous Moon

A peach was the first fruit eaten on the Moon.

The Moon orbits the Earth once every 27.32 days, which is just under a month.

Dr Dino's Did You Know?

The tidal action of the Moon's pull slows the Earth down by 2.2 seconds every 100,000 years or so. In fact, 600,000,000 years ago, back when my first ancestors were floating around in the sea, our day would have been only around 22 hours long and in another 600,000,000 it will be 26 hours long.

Neil Armstrong might have been the first man to walk on the Moon, but Buzz Aldrin gets the far greater honour of being the first man to pee his pants on the Moon!

The only person to play golf on the Moon was Alan Shepherd. His golf balls have never been found.

A full moon always rises at sunset and is 11 times brighter than a quarter moon.

Gigantic Grub

Every year thousands of farmers, both professional and amateur, around the world compete to see who can grow the biggest food, with competitions in everything from who has the biggest potato to the biggest turnip. Here are just a few of the all-time records:

In October 2013 Tim Mathison set a new world record at the 23rd Annual Giant Pumpkin Weigh-Off in California with a pumpkin weighing a gigantic 2,032 pounds. That's about the same as a fully-grown walrus and heavier than

some elephants. The pumpkin was taken to New York to do a series of TV events.

The world's heaviest apple, by contrast, weighed in at 'only' 4 pounds and 1 ounce. It was picked by apple farmer Chisato Iwasaki at his farm in Japan.

Chris Kent, an accountant from Tennessee, proved he wasn't too boring when he grew the world's largest watermelon in October 2013. He beat the previous record by 42.5 pounds when the watermelon was revealed to be 350.5 pounds. A single seed from that watermelon was valued at about £10 and it had around 1,500 seeds, making it by far the world's most expensive watermelon.

The largest cabbage ever grown weighed 138.25 pounds. It was grown by Scott Robb and presented at the Alaska State Fair in 2012. The next year, in 2013, the competition was won by 10-year-old Keevan Dinkel.

The UK held the world record for the world's longest cucumber at 47 inches long. However that was smashed by a young farmer in China who grew a 5 foot 7 inch long cucumber. It was bigger than him! The secret? He used horse poo to help it grow.

Wonderful Words

If you want to impress your friends and teachers, try slipping in some of these words into everyday conversation. There are 26 here, one for each letter of the alphabet:

An **armsaye** is the word for the armhole in clothing.

The skin that peels off you after you get sunburned is called **blype**.

Food that has just been spat out is called **chanking**.

A **deltiologist** is someone who collects postcards.

Ejectamenta is the word for everything that comes spewing out of a volcano.

A **funambulist** is another name for a tightrope walker.

Watching people eating in the hope that they will offer you some of it is called **groaking**.

A **horologist** measures time.

When you are afraid of going to the doctors you have **iatrophobia**.

Jazzetry is the official name for poetry when it is read out accompanied by some lovely jazz music.

The word **karate** mean 'empty hand'.

The white area at the base of a fingernail is called the **lunula**.

If you are **macrocephalic** you have a very large head.

The next time you're told it's your bedtime, tell your parents that you are a **noceur**. That's someone who naturally stays up late.

Another word for your armpit is an **oxter**.

When you yawn I bet you **pandiculate,** which is the way you stretch your body when you yawn.

Quagswag has nothing to do with swag. It is the act of shaking back and forth.

The habit of picking your nose is called **rhinotillexomania**.

A Sultan's wife is called a **Sultana**. She shouldn't be confused with a grape, dried or otherwise.

The single dot over the letter i is called a **tittle**.

If something is slimy it can be described as **uliginous**.

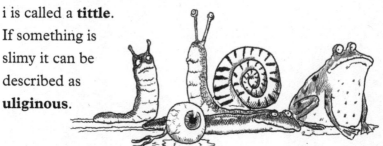

29

To **vaticinate** is to predict the future, like a prophet.

Unsurprisingly, someone who goes to a wedding is officially called a **weddinger**.

Xenologists would say that they study the extraterrestrial. Everyone else would just say that they believe in aliens.

A **youf** is a woof that has been muffled in some way.

If you are a **zoilist** you are someone who enjoys finding fault in things.

Deep Space

You could be forgiven for thinking that the Earth isn't moving – but actually it's moving very quickly indeed. In fact, it's speeding around the Sun at a ridiculous 66,600 miles per hour. And on top of that, it spins on its axis at roughly 1,000 miles per hour. When you think about it, it's amazing you don't feel dizzy.

Our galaxy, the Milky Way, contains at least 100,000,000,000 stars, and may have up to 400,000,000,000. To give a sense of perspective, if the Milky Way were the size of a 100-metre running track, our solar system would be about the same size as a grain of sand!

If that doesn't make you feel small, although scientists don't really know how many galaxies there are in the Universe, their best guess is that there are 100,000,000,000. Which means that they think there might be around 70 sextillion stars. If you're wondering how many zeros that is, it's an awful lot: 70,000,000,000,000,000,000,000.

Dr Dino's Did You Know?

If you're an American astronaut and want to vote for the President I'm afraid that's too bad – unless you're from Texas, which is the only state in America that allows you to vote in space.

The Universe is about 13.8 billion years old. The Earth is only about a third as old as that, at around 4.54 billion years old.

Scientists believe that the Universe isn't finite. That means it just keeps expanding and becoming bigger and bigger.

What it is expanding into, nobody knows. But if you think about it enough, it makes your head hurt. A lot.

Once known as the ninth planet in our Solar System, Pluto, about two-thirds the size of our Moon, was declassified as a planet in 2006 and named a dwarf planet. And, in fact, it's not even the biggest dwarf planet in the solar system, as Eris, a dwarf planet discovered in 2005, is actually 27% larger than Pluto.

Loony Laws From Around the World

Every citizen of Kentucky, USA, is required by law to take a bath at least once a year.

In Tibet, China, all Buddhist monks are banned from reincarnating after they die – unless they first get government permission!

Elsewhere in the USA, in Hartford, Connecticut, you may not, under any circumstances, cross the street walking on your hands.

A law in Virginia, USA, requires all bathtubs to be kept out in the garden, not inside the house.

It is strictly forbidden to stare at the Mayor of Paris.

Back in the USA, in Omaha, Nebraska, it's against the law to burp or sneeze in church.

Dr Dino's Most Dangerous Law

The next time you forget to revise for a test and copy off a friend instead, feel grateful you don't live in Bangladesh. It is against the law to cheat in school there, and if you're caught you can be thrown in jail! Maybe detention isn't so bad after all...

In Sweden it is illegal to train a seal to balance a ball on its nose.

In the US state of Texas you are not allowed to put graffiti on someone else's cow.

In Alabama you are not allowed to wrestle bears. The US state law doesn't give advice on what to do if you come across a bear that wants to wrestle.

Not-so-ingenious
Inventions

Inventors have changed the way you humans live your lives, from the caveman who first came up with the spear, to the most famous inventor of all-time, Leonardo da Vinci, who back in the late 15th and early 16th centuries came up with designs for a helicopter, a tank, and even built a robotic knight! But not all inventions have worked so well, and here are a few of the more bizarre:

5. In the 1930s members of the Chelsea Baby Club, who often had small apartments, were given baby cages. This doesn't sound too bad, except that they weren't designed for indoors. To save room they were attached to the outside of a window and dangled over the edge!

4. In 1948 a man called Joe Gilpin invented a motorised surfboard. While fine for travelling very slowly around lakes, it didn't work well at all when it came across a wave, which kind of misses the point of surfing.

3. A curved machine-gun was developed in the 1950s for shooting around corners. Unfortunately, this had the obvious drawback of not letting the soldier see where he was shooting...

2. You might have 3D TV glasses at home, but Hugo Gernsback was ahead of the game in 1963 when he invented the original TV glasses. These were actually just glasses with a very small, but heavy, TV attached to them.

1. However, the prize for the worst invention of all time has to go to Henry Smolinski's flying car. In 1973, Smolinski strapped the wings of a Cessna airplane to a Ford Pinto and went for a test 'flight'. He did manage to take off, but unfortunately

the car quickly broke free and fell to Earth, killing
Smolinski and his unlucky passenger.

Dr Dino's Favourite Inventors

Alexander Graham Bell, who invented the telephone,
never called his wife or mother. They were both deaf.
And Thomas Edison, the inventor of the light bulb,
was afraid of the dark.

What's in a Name?
Part 1

The human with the longest name in the world is Adolph Blaine Charles David Earl Frederick Gerald Hubert Irvin John Kenneth Lloyd Martin Nero Oliver Paul Quincy Randolph Sherman Thomas Uncas Victor William Xerxes Yancy Zeus Wolfeschlegelsteinhausenbergerdorft Senior. One name for each letter of the alphabet. However, even that is an abbreviation, because his last name was apparently actually: Wolfeschlegelsteinhausenbergerdorffvoralternwarengewissenhaftschaferswessenschafewarenwohlgepflegeundsorgfaltigkeitbeschutzenvonangreifendurchihrraubgierigfeindewelchevoralternzwolftausendjahresvorandieerscheinenwanderersteerdemenschderraumschiffgebrauchlichtalsseinursprungvonkraftgestarteinlangefahrthinzwischensternartigraumaufdersuchenachdiesternwelchegehabtbewohnbarplanetenkreisedrehensichundwohinderneurassevonverstandigmenschlichkeitkonntefortplanzenundsicherfreuenanlebenslanglichfreudeundruhemit-

nichteinfurchtvorangreifenvonandererintelligentge-
schopfsvonhinzwischensternartigraum.
Imagine having to write that before every exam!

Muhammad is the most common name in the world meaning that, on average, the most common name in the UK is Muhammad Smith.

Dr Dino's Did You Know?

In the UK, surnames as we use them only developed in the 13th and 14th centuries. They were given because of distinctive features – so if your last name is Cook or Smith, your ancestor was most likely a cook or a smith. Or if your last name is Jameson, your ancestor was probably the 'son of James'.

If you visit Asia, you should never write anyone's names in red. When a death certificate is being written, red ink is always used. If you write someone's name in red, it means you want them dead!

London Underground

The London Underground first opened with the Metropolitan Line in 1863 which used steam trains to pull gas-lit wooden carriages along. It was a huge success, but as you can imagine the air got pretty dirty down there! When the Circle Line opened in 1884, the *Times* described it as 'a form of mild torture'.

Aldgate station is built over an old plague pit... And there are at least 1,000 bodies beneath it from the 17th century! Ugh.

There are dozens of old disused stations on the Underground. Some have been demolished, but many just sit there as ghost stations. One of them – Down Street – was used by Churchill as a bunker in World War II.

Dr Dino's Did You Know?

The Russian word for railway station is 'vokzal'. It supposedly came from a visiting 19th-century Russian who visited Vauxhall in London, and took the word back with him.

The Tube's lost property office has looked after some pretty weird things. To name a few, people have left a samurai sword, a human skull and a coffin on the Tube network before. How forgetful!

The Tube is most famous for its catchphrase 'Mind the Gap' (referring to the gap between train and platform). They still play the original recording of it at Embankment – the powers-that-be restored it after the recorder's widow wrote in to ask if they could play it again because she wanted to hear his voice.

Ironic Deaths

Clement Vallandigham was a lawyer who was defending someone accused of murdering someone else. His defence was that the dead person had accidentally shot himself while drawing his own gun. That sounds unlikely, so Vallandigham, in what was either the best or worst move by a lawyer ever, demonstrated how it could happen and *accidentally shot himself!* He later died, but the jury was convinced and the man he was defending was found innocent…

Bobby Leach was a daredevil who was most famous for throwing himself down the Niagara Falls and surviving (although he did break his jaw and his kneecaps), among many other hair-raising stunts. One day, he was walking down a road and slipped on some orange-peel. He later died from wounds he got in the fall. So he survived falling 180 feet down a waterfall, but not tripping over.

Segways, the two-wheeled motor-scooters, were invented by Jimi Heselden, who made more than £100 million from them. However, he was out for a spin on his Segway one day when he lost control and drove straight over an 80-foot cliff.

Legend has it that Aeschylus, one of the greatest playwrights of the ancient Greeks, was warned that he would die one day from something falling on his head. Naturally, he tried to stay out in the open for as much time as he could. However, one day an eagle, thinking his bald head was a rock, dropped a turtle on him in an attempt to smash the turtle's shell. Instead, it smashed Aeschylus's head and killed him. Happily, the turtle survived.

Football Fanatics

The football fan with the worst luck was Pedro Gatica, who cycled all the way from Argentina to Mexico – around 4,600 miles – in 1986 to watch the World Cup. When he got there he found that the tickets were too expensive for him to get in and, to make things worse, while he was bartering for a ticket someone stole his bike!

Ion Radu was sold in 1998 from Jiul Petrosani to Valcea in Romania – for 500 kilograms of pork.

Willie 'Fatty' Foulke has the privilege of being the heaviest-ever England player. He played for England as a goalkeeper in 1897 and weighed in at over 22 stones. He would be classified as obese now!

Dr Dino's Did You Know?

Nobody knows who invented football (the first reference to it in England was in the ninth century), but in the early Middle Ages it used to be played between whole villages with very few rules – the 'game' was so violent that it was quite common for people to die during matches! It was so bad that in 1314 King Edward III tried to ban football because it was too violent. Clearly, he wasn't very successful.

The most goals scored, and conceded, in one match was 149. In Madagascar, AS Adema beat Stade Olympique l'Emyrne 149-0, but they didn't even score a goal. Stade were so angry at a refereeing decision that they protested by scoring 149 own goals – thus becoming the side to both score and concede the most goals.

Karl Power is a huge Manchester United fan and went one step further than most to prove it. In 2001 he dressed in the Man Utd kit and tricked security into thinking he was part of the team, managing to walk out onto the pitch with the players and even getting into the team photo!

In 2006 in São Paulo, Brazil, Atletico Sorocaba were leading Santacruzense 1-0 in the final minutes, when Santacruzense had a shot just go wide. The referee awarded a goal kick and turned around. While she looked away a cheeky ball boy ran out and 'scored'. The ref turned back, saw the ball in the net, and awarded a goal. Atletico were incensed, but the goal stood, and the ball boy became a hero. The ref, meanwhile, faced a suspension.

Plants You Don't Want in Your Garden

Skunk cabbage is a plant which does exactly what it says in the name – it smells like a skunk, and is probably the worst-smelling plant on the planet.

The Australian Gympie-Gympie tree might have a funny name, but it is a deadly serious plant. It can claim to be the world's most deadly tree, and it puts stinging nettles to shame. When it stings you, the poison is so strong that, if it doesn't kill you straight away, it keeps hurting for two whole years.

The Venus flytrap is the most famous of the carnivorous plants – that is, plants that eat meat. It works by detecting when something living is touching it and then snapping its leaves shut in a tenth of a second, trapping whatever is unlucky enough to be on it. There are many other plants like this around the world, but luckily none of them are big enough to eat much more than insects.

Dr Dino's Did You Know?

There are a number of references in ancient stories to the sea turning a terrifying red – like blood. This phenomenon, called the Red Tide, can be explained by a far more boring cause than blood though. Algae. Tonnes of it. So much that it changes the colour of the water. However, the results aren't so boring. Some of this algae is very toxic and paralyses limbs, so swimming in the Red Tide can be a very dangerous experience indeed. Occasionally it kills all of the fish that swim through it, and millions of dead fish wash up onto shore.

The Earth Moves

As you're reading this, 20 volcanoes are erupting. Yes, right now! The majority of volcanoes are underwater, however, and erupt very slowly with no damage to people.

The biggest earthquake in recorded history was in May 1960 in Chile. It recorded 9.5 on the Richter scale and caused huge damage. It also created a tsunami that travelled all the way across the Pacific Ocean, devastating places as far away as Hawaii and Japan with huge 10-metre waves.

Even the biggest volcanic eruptions in modern times have been pretty tame. Every so often a supervolcano erupts, and then things get really bad. The last time this happened was when Toba erupted in Indonesia about 75,000 years ago – it caused a mini ice-age and almost killed off the human race!

Dr Dino's Did You Know?

Volcanoes and earthquakes are caused by the movement of tectonic plates, which are the huge slabs of rock that make up the Earth's crust. Because these are always moving, the surface of the Earth is constantly in motion. For 100,000,000 years the Earth had just one huge continent, called Pangaea, and then 200,000,000 years ago, when all my friends were roaming around the planet, it started splitting up, slowly becoming the world we know today. Scientists have predicted that in 100,000,000 years we will have another supercontinent, called Amasia, but this one will form over the North Pole. So the world could be pretty chilly!

There are two earthquakes every minute in the world. The overwhelming majority are so small only the most sensitive equipment can feel them.

Pompeii was an Ancient Roman town that was destroyed when Mount Vesuvius erupted in AD 79. The town was covered by tonnes of ash and was perfectly preserved as it was in the moment it was covered, until it was found in the 18th century. Pompeii is still being excavated, but it now looks exactly like it did 2,000 years ago – except that it's full of tourists!

Our Home Planet

Each year about 40,000 tonnes of meteorites and space debris lands on the Earth, mostly in the form of dust.

Dr Dino's Did You Know?

The Earth isn't round, it is what's called an 'oblate spheroid' meaning it is flattened at the poles and bulging at the equator. Because the equator is further from the centre of the Earth, gravity there is slightly less than it is on the poles. So if you weigh 150 pounds on the equator, you will weigh 151 pounds on the North Pole.

The Earth has a powerful magnetic field. This allows us to survive – without it, solar winds (radiation from the Sun) would ravage the Earth and kill all life very quickly.

Earth is the only planet that we know of that has water on it. Without it, life would be impossible.

If you've ever tried to dig a hole through the centre of the Earth to the other side: STOP! The centre of the Earth, called the 'inner core' is very hot. In fact, it's as hot as the Sun, at about 5,400 degrees Celsius.

About 70% of the Earth is covered with water. Although we think of the world as being completely discovered now, and most of the land-surface is, humans have only explored about 5% of the ocean floor. To a large extent, nobody knows what's in the ocean!

You would need a tape measure 24,902 miles long to measure right around the world. On average, a human walks far enough in their lifetime to go around the world 4.5 times.

Amazing Architecture

The tallest building in the world is the Burj Khalifa in Dubai at a ridiculous 829.8 metres, which is about 200 metres taller than the next biggest man-made structure, and it has 58 elevators in it.

The Shard in London is the tallest in Europe but only 62nd in the world. At 306 metres, it's only just over a third of the size of the Burj Khalifa.

The Great Wall of China is so long that nobody really knows how long it is. A survey has concluded that the Wall is about 5,500 miles long. However, if you include all of the branches of the wall with its natural defences, it's more like 13,171 miles long.

Dr Dino's Did You Know?

The Great Wall of China might be the world's longest wall, but Australia completed something to rival it in 1885... the world's longest fence. It is 3,488 miles long, and is designed to keep out dingoes – in fact it's called the Dingo Fence.

In Sopot, Poland you can find one of the world's oddest houses. It is called The Crooked House, and it is designed to look like you are looking at it through water.

There is an old woman who lives in a shoe... in Hellam, Pennsylvania where a shoe salesman has built a house that looks exactly like a shoe. Bizarrely, it is now an ice cream shop.

In 2013 a curved skyscraper in London caused unexpected problems when the Sun's rays reflected off the windows and focused on one spot – a car. The heat was so strong that parts of the car actually melted.

Brilliant Books

Many writers, including Charles Dickens and Virginia Wolfe, preferred to write their books standing up. I wrote this standing up, but not out of choice. Your human chairs are far too small for me. If anyone can design a chair that will fit me I would very much appreciate it.

The Adventures of Tom Sawyer was the first book written on a typewriter.

Sherlock Holmes never said 'Elementary, my dear Watson' in any of the books by Sir Arthur Conan Doyle.

The final book in the Harry Potter series became the fastest-selling book of all time when, just on the first day of publication, it sold 15,000,000 copies worldwide.

In 1955 a book about the Archbishop of Bremen was returned to Cambridge University Library. It was 288 years overdue! Luckily, the library decided not to make them pay the fine.

There are approximately 2,200,000 books published around the world each year. No library in the world could hold all of the books published so far in the 21st century.

When Charles Darwin first published his famous book, *Origin of Species*, his publisher suggested if he wanted it to be popular he should include more information about pigeons. Because everyone likes pigeons.

The world's most expensive book ever bought was the *Codex Leicester* by Leonardo da Vinci. Bill Gates, co-founder of Microsoft, bought it in 1994 for $30,802,500.

Get to Know Yourself

Everyone has individual finger (or claw) prints – except for identical twins, who also have identical fingerprints.

The average person blinks more than 6,000,000 times per year. And that's a blinking fact!

Your brain is more active when you are asleep than it is when you are watching TV. Humans have five different dreams on average per night.

Farts have been timed and can come out at a rapid 10 metres per second. If you could fart continuously for six years and nine months, you would have produced as much energy as an atomic bomb!

Dr Dino's Favourite Flatulent Fact
There is an Indian tribe in South America called the Yanomami who say hello by farting at each other!

One human foot contains 250,000 sweat glands, and there are also about 1,000,000,000,000 bacteria on each foot. No wonder they smell so bad!

Reading about yawning makes most people yawn.........
See?

Faster than the Speed of Light?

Nothing in the Universe – that we know of – is faster than light. It travels at 299,792,458 metres per second, which means it can travel right around the Earth 7.4 times in just one second.

Usain Bolt is the fastest man who has ever lived. In 2009, he ran the 100 metres in Berlin in 9.58 seconds, a time that wasn't thought humanly possible 10 years before.

Dr Dino's Did You Know?

The faster you go, the slower time goes. Einstein's theory of special relativity is so confusing that you have to be... well... Einstein to figure out what he was talking about. But he showed that when you move, time goes slower for you than for everyone standing still. If you are travelling at 40 miles per hour, time only goes 0.0000000000000002% slower, which isn't much at all. However, if you were in orbit and travelled for one year at the speed of light, 22 years would pass on Earth! There is even a theory that, if you could travel faster than light, you could possibly turn back time!

The land speed record was set in 1997 by Brit Andy Green. He travelled one mile at a speed of 763.035 miles per hour, breaking the speed of sound. Fortunately, no policemen were there to catch him for speeding!

On 14 October 2012 Felix Baumgartner did something nobody else has ever achieved – he broke the sound barrier without the help of any machine. Felix went up in a specially made balloon to the height of 38,969.3 metres (that's right on the edge of space) and jumped. He hit a top speed of 843.6 miles per hour, which is faster than most airplanes. Just before he jumped he said 'I'm going home now.'

A Sporting Life

The sport played by the most amount of people around the world isn't football. It's fishing, or to be precise, angling. The term angling indicates that the fish has to be caught on a hook rather than in a net.

First-class cricket matches can last up to five days nowadays. But before a limit was set they could go on until a result was reached. The longest-ever Test match started on 3 March 1939 when England began playing against South Africa in Durban. It finished 12 days later – but as a draw. England found themselves stumped before they could actually finish the contest – they had to leave or they would miss their boat back home!

The most dangerous sport in the world is… lawn bowls. More people die playing bowls every year than any other sport – mainly because most of the players are so old that they have heart attacks during the matches.

Tiger Woods is the highest paid sportsman in the world. In 2012 he earned $86,000,000 – $13,000,000 from his winnings and a massive $73,000,000 from his sponsors. That was actually a pay cut from 2009 when he made a world-record $122,000,000!

The strings in tennis rackets are sometimes called guts. This is because they used to actually be made out of sheep and cows guts!

French rugby player Gaston Vareilles was picked to play against Scotland in 1910. The team took a train across France and, while they were stopped at Lyon, he decided to run to the station buffet for a sandwich. Unfortunately, the queue was so long that by the time he got his snack the train had already left. He didn't make it to the match in time and he was never picked for France again.

The first time a national anthem was sung before a sport's match was in 1905 when Welsh selector Tom Williams decided that Wales should sing it in response to New Zealand's Haka. Now anthems are sung before every international in most sports.

The Olympics

The Ancient Greeks used to hold the Olympics but the Games were halted in the year AD 393, having started all the way back in 776 BC. The event was restarted in 1896, about 1,500 years later.

The colours of the Olympic rings – yellow, green, red, black and blue – represent every colour that appears in a national flag around the world.

Dr Dino's Did You Know?

Gold medals aren't actually gold. They are silver with a gold plating. The last time they were solid gold was in 1912, but after that it was decided it would be too expensive to make that many gold medals.

In 1900 the Dutch rowing team needed a cox (the person who sits at the front of the boat and yells at the team when to row) right before the race, so they pulled a young boy out of the crowd. He did well – so well that they won! He posed for the team photo and then ran off, and was never heard of again. To this day, nobody knows who he was, but he is believed to be the youngest medallist ever.

The first American woman to win gold in the Olympics didn't even realise she had done so. In 1900 Margaret Abbott saw an advert in a magazine for a golf tournament, entered and won it. She went home with a porcelain bowl for a prize without ever being told she was competing in the Olympics.

Michael Phelps, an American swimmer, has the best medals tally in Olympics history, having won 22 between 2004 and 2012. Amazingly, 18 of those 22 were gold! The champion swimmer is known for having a huge appetite and starts the day with three egg sandwiches, three chocolate chip pancakes, a five-egg omelette, three slices of sugary French toast and, to top it off, a bowl of porridge. If he thinks that's a lot he should see what I have for breakfast...

World's Biggest and Best

The world's oldest goldfish lived to be 43 years old. His name was Tish and he was buried with full honours in a yoghurt carton at the bottom of his owner's garden.

Despite their calm appearance, the most common name for a goldfish is Jaws.

The largest yo-yo in the world weighs an unbelievable 3,300 kilograms. Unsurprisingly, nobody can use it unless they have a crane, but then it works perfectly.

Donna Griffiths holds the unfortunate record for the world's longest sneezing fit. She began sneezing on 13 January 1981 and a year later she was still going, having sneezed about 1,000,000 times. Her first sneeze-free day came an astounding 978 days later! There was no record of how many tissues she got through...

Donna had it easy compared to Charles Osborne though. He started hiccupping in 1922 and continued for 68 years until 1980, averaging about 40 hiccups a minute!

The biggest hamburger ever made was on 2 September 2012 in Minnesota when Black Bear Casino Resort prepared a hamburger weighing 913 kilograms. In case that wasn't filling enough, they topped it with over 100 kilograms of extras, including 23.8 kilograms of tomatoes, 18.1 kilograms of cheese and 7.5 kilograms of bacon.

The largest living thing on Earth isn't a whale. It's a tree called General Sherman which is 83.8 metres tall and probably about 2,000 years old.

Odd Body

Most people's legs are slightly different lengths, but your body gets used to it, so you don't notice.

Fingernails are made from the same substance as a bird's beak, hard keratin.

During your lifetime, you will produce enough saliva to fill two whole swimming pools.

Right-handed people tend to chew food on the right side of their mouths, and vice versa for left-handed people.

Everybody is about one centimetre taller in the morning than in the evening. This is because as you sleep you stretch yourself out, but during the day the pressure on your knees and other joints (because of your weight) is so great that you slightly compress.

About 300,000,000 cells die in your body every minute. Fortunately, your body is constantly building new ones to replenish them.

The longest time anyone has ever stayed awake was 11 days. By the end of it, the sleepyhead was stumbling over words, hallucinating and kept on forgetting what he was doing.

Your brain is what allows you to feel pain, as your nerves send impulses up to your brain. Ironically, the only part of your body that can't feel pain is... your brain.

Foreign Foods

In the USA the average American eats 756 doughnuts every year. That's more than two a day.

There is a Museum of Spaghetti in Pontedassio, Italy. It was founded in 1956 and probably the strangest exhibit is a will from 1279 in which an Italian soldier leaves a basket of spaghetti to his heir.

In many African countries termites – which are like large, white ants – are eaten. In some areas they are roasted and eaten like popcorn, and in others they are mixed in with bread and porridge for flavour and protein.

Dr Dino's Did You Know?

One of the most-eaten foods around the world was invented in England, not by a chef, but by a man called the Earl of Sandwich. He came up with a simple snack because he loved playing cards and didn't want to take a break just to have lunch. So he ordered his servants to bring him his food in between two slabs of bread; a culinary phenomenon – the sandwich – was born.

The famous haggis, which is Scotland's national dish, is made from mixing the 'offal' (parts of the animal like the heart, lungs and liver) of sheep with other stuff such as suet and oatmeal and then putting it all inside of the stomach of the sheep to cook. Bon appétit!

In Cambodia, fried spiders are considered a real delicacy. And if you want to really impress a guest, you would serve them a deep-fried tarantula.

If you ever find yourself in Mexico, be careful not to order escamoles. They may look like delicious white beans, but they are in fact giant ant's eggs. Apparently eating them is a bit like eating cottage cheese... only a lot more disgusting.

Tiet Cahn, when refrigerated, looks a little bit like jelly. You wouldn't want to serve this up with ice cream though. It is a traditional Vietnamese dish with very few ingredients. In fact, it's mainly just one – raw blood. Yuk!

Spacemanimals

Before humans boldly went where nobody had gone before – space – something actually did go before them. The first astronauts weren't people at all, but a group of brave animals that made space travel possible. Here are the stories of a few of them:

The first animals in space weren't really animals but insects. Fruit flies to be exact. They were sent out of our atmosphere by the USA on 20 February 1947 and came back to Earth alive.

In 1951 a pair of Russian dogs, Tsygan and Dezik, became the first big animals to survive in space, proving it was possible – before that many thought it couldn't be done.

Albert II had the honour in 1949 of being the first monkey in space. Sadly, after making it 83 miles up in the air he

came back to Earth with a bit too much of a bang – the parachute failed and Albert II died when he landed.

Many other animals have been sent into space, including cats, rabbits, mice, frogs, rats, guinea pigs, wasps, beetles, tortoises, fish, spiders, stick insects, newts, scorpions, worms, cockroaches and butterflies. And, of course, humans. No dinosaurs – yet.

Belka and Strelka were a couple of Russian dogs who became the first dogs to survive in orbit in space. Strelka later had pups and one of them was given to the daughter of the US President, Caroline Kennedy. She took really good care of it, and today there are many, many descendants running around all over America.

Sensational Senses

Your sense of smell has been proven to be linked strongly with your emotions. For example, when they smell crayons, 85% of humans have strong flashbacks to their childhood.

Although you've probably been told there are five senses (touch, taste, sight, smell and hearing) that's not the end of it. The famous Greek philosopher Aristotle was the first to name those five senses, but since then they have been updated and there are anywhere between nine and 21 or so, depending on who you talk to. Here are just a few of the ones you probably won't have thought about:

Itch – How itchy we are is nothing to do with our other touching sensitivity.
Time – Even without a clock we are generally able to tell pretty well how much time has passed. And this is

why your 'body clock' gets messed up by jetlag when you travel.

Proprioception – This fancy word just means that you can always tell where your body is in relation to the rest of your body. Without it, you wouldn't even be able to clap your hands.

Thermoception – This one actually counts as two senses, and it is the ability of your body to detect heat (or cold). One sense is external, for how hot or cold it is outside your body, and one is internal, for your own body's temperature. When you are ill with a fever, it is this sense that tells you something is wrong.

Taste is actually mostly smell. If you couldn't smell anything at all, you wouldn't be able to tell the difference between an onion, a potato, an apple or even a strawberry.

Dr Dino's Did You Know?

The world record for human vision was set by Dr Dennis Levi in 1985 – he was able to spot a line a quarter of an inch thick from a mile away.

Unlike your sense of smell, which turns off when you are asleep, you continue to hear things 24/7. This is why you will sometimes wake with a start if there's a loud bang, but not if someone's just done a smelly fart next to you!

Everything you see goes to your brain upside down, and then your brain flips the vision the right way up. George Stratton was a scientist who came up with the idea that if he wore glasses that made him see everything upside down, he could trick his brain into not changing the image. It worked and after eight days of the experiment his brain had adjusted and he could see everything normally. The only problem was, when he took the glasses off, the whole world looked like it was upside down to him for a few days!

The Royal Windsors

The Queen of England is incredibly lucky – she gets to have two birthdays. One's real, which is on 21 April, and the other is her 'official' one, which is celebrated publicly and is always on a Saturday in June.

The Royal Family belong to the House of Windsor (basically meaning that's their surname), but they weren't always called that. Before the First World War the Royal Family were of the House of Saxe-Coburg and Gotha, but that's a German name and during the war people disliked the Germans so much that they decided to change it to something a little more English...

The Queen has what must be the world's most annoying alarm clock. Whenever she is staying at one of her main great residences (Buckingham Palace, Windsor Castle, Holyrood or Balmoral) a bagpiper opens up for a full 15 minutes at 9am. And no matter how hard you try, he won't shut up!

Prince Charles likes his comforts while he travels, and none more so than on the loo. He refuses to go anywhere without his own white leather personal toilet seat!

Dr Dino's Did You Know?

You probably don't know the names of all of the Kings and Queens of England, even if you think you do. In fact, the names we know them by are their reigning names, not necessarily their real ones. Queen Victoria was actually called Princess Alexandrina. Prince Charles isn't expected to be King Charles either when he succeeds his mother, but will most likely be King George VII.

Prince Philip is much-loved both by his wife, the Queen, and by the British people. He does, however, have the habit of saying the wrong thing at the wrong time. For example, after once being told that Madonna was going to sing the next James Bond theme tune he asked 'Are we going to need ear plugs?' And to the President of Nigeria, who was wearing traditional clothes which looked a tiny bit like pyjamas, he said 'You look like you're ready for bed.'

Buckingham Palace has an unbelievable 775 rooms. During World War II the Palace was bombed by the Germans and was hit nine times. Quite often King George VI and his wife (and our Queen's mother) Elizabeth were in the Palace and narrowly missed being killed. In fact, only one person perished – a policeman called Steve Robertson, who has a plaque on display in the gardens to appreciate him.

Micro
Science

Everything in the world is made up of atoms, and they are pretty small. The average human is thought to contain 7,000,000,000,000,000,000,000,000,000 atoms, which you'll agree is quite a lot!

Atoms might be small, but they are still pretty empty. In fact, 99.9999999999999% of an atom is just space. If you could get rid of all of the space and squish them together, the entire human race would be able to be squashed down to fit fairly easily into a sugar cube. It would be pretty heavy though – that cube would probably weigh about 5,000,000,000 tonnes!

Dr Dino's Did You Know?

The smallest known thing in the Universe is something called a quark. It is the building block that makes up atoms and it is so small that there is no way to measure its size. All you can say is that one quark is about the size of... one quark.

The smallest particles in the Universe, like quarks, are all spinning and all have twins. Bizarrely, if one of those twins is spinning clockwise, the other has to be spinning anti-clockwise. Somehow, no matter how far away they are, even if the particles are on the other side of the world, they know what the other one is doing and if one changes direction, so will the other!

All of the atoms in the world are constantly recycled. The chances are that some of the atoms that make you were at some point part of Shakespeare.

They might be tiny, but they are pretty powerful. When atoms are split, they give off a fair amount of energy and it was 'splitting the atom' that led to the greatest man-made explosions in war of all-time – the nuclear bombs that the US dropped on Japan at the end of the Second World War.

Do you know your ABCs?

The largest alphabet in the world is the Khmer alphabet in Cambodia. It is 74 letters long, and some of them aren't even used anymore. It's a lot harder to play Scrabble there!

In English the most commonly used letter is E, while the least used is Q. The most common word is unsurprisingly 'the', which I've already used three times in this fact. Oops, make that four!

Inancientgreecetherewasnopunctuationorspaceinbe-tweenwordsitjustlookedlikethisimaginehowhardthis-musthavebeentoread (In ancient Greece there was no punctuation or space in between words, it just looked like this. Imagine how hard this must have been to read). Could you have read that? Would you be able to if there were pages and pages just like that? Grammar might be boring, but it's very important!

Dr Dino's Did You Know?

English has a lot more words than any other Western language, like Italian or German. This is because the language Old English was Germanic in origin as the Anglo-Saxons came from around Germany. But when the Vikings arrived in the 9th and 10th centuries they brought a lot of Norse words with them (such as die, cake, hit, window), and then the Normans introduced many French and Latin words (like dagger, farce, grand, isle) when they conquered England in 1066. Because of this, the English language has more words to choose from than any other, at least in Europe.

The letter W is the only letter in the English alphabet to have more than one syllable – it has three. The longest one-syllable word is 'screeched'.

The shortest alphabet in the world is the Rotokas alphabet which is only 11 letters long. It is spoken by about 4,000 people in Bougainville, an island that is part of Papua New Guinea.

It's believed that there are about 7,000 different languages in the world. Most of these barely have any speakers, with very few dominating the world.

There are 46 languages in the world that have only one user! Conversations with them can become very dull very quickly.

Strange Sports

At school everyone plays the same sports (football, netball, cricket, rugby, hockey, velociraptor toss) and if you're not too good at them you might think that is the end of your sporting career. But don't worry, there are a lot of crazy sports out there for you to try. Here are 10 of the weirdest:

10. Extreme Ironing: this sport is basically ironing in dangerous places. According to the Extreme Ironing Bureau, Extreme Ironing is 'the latest danger sport that combines the thrills of an extreme outdoor activity with the satisfaction of a well-pressed shirt'. Places where it has been played include on parachute dives and under the ice cover of a lake.

9. Chess Boxing: it's fairly simple to figure this one out. It's chess and boxing combined. The competitors go 11 rounds (six playing chess and five boxing) and the winner

is the one who either gets a checkmate first or knocks the other person out first.

8. Elephant Polo: exactly the same as polo, except played on elephants. You don't want to fall off!

7. Zorbing: invented in Rotorua in New Zealand, the participants get into huge plastic balls and then set off down a big hill. The fastest to roll to the bottom, wins. Variations can be played such as zorbing football where you play football as normal, but while inside a zorb.

6. Giant Pumpkin Kayaking: half the challenge of this sport is finding a pumpkin big enough and then carving it out to make a 'kayak'. Once you've done that, the rest is easy.

5. Bog Snorkelling: the Welsh sport of bog-snorkelling is a fiercely competitive one. Competitors swim underwater through peat bogs with the help of a snorkel and goggles, but they are only allowed to use their legs. Bog Snorkelling is part of the wider World Alternative Games, which also includes such sports as the Bible Readathon, Finger Jousting, the Office Chair Slalom, the Russian Egg Roulette and Wife Carrying.

4. Worm Charming: this is all about using vibrations to lure worms out of the ground. There are very strict rules about what you can and can't do to get them out (you can't just dig), but the person with the largest number of worms collected wins.

3. Cheese Rolling: during this Gloucestershire sport someone rolls a nine-pound wheel of cheese down a very big, very steep hill, and the 'racers' sprint down the hill after it. The hill is so steep though that the competitors really just end up trying to fall down it in the fastest, least

painful way they can. And what's the prize? The block of cheese of course!

2. Mud-pit Belly Flop: the only thing you need for this sport is a big muddy puddle and someone stupid enough to want to belly flop into it. Prizes go for the biggest splash on impact, so if you're a spectator, you might want to stand well back!

1. Outhouse Racing: this sport takes port-a-potties one step too far. The rules are your outhouse must have a toilet and toilet paper dispenser inside and be mounted on skis. Two people can push and two people pull to get it started, and then it's downhill for the rider, who is inside. The toilet doesn't have to flush, so whatever happens, you don't want the outhouse to fall over!

Dinosaurs – The Greatest Creatures that Ever Lived

My fellow dinosaurs were around for 165 million years, making us history's most successful rulers of the world – and don't you forget it! Modern humans have only existed for around 200,000 years so you have a bit of a way to go yet before you last as long as us.

About 66 million years ago, during the saddest, most devastating time the world has ever seen, almost all of the dinosaurs on Earth suddenly became extinct, along with many of the other living things alongside us. Scientists have a couple of theories as to why – either a massive series of volcanic eruptions or a huge asteroid hitting Earth and causing enormous devastation. I'd be happy to let them know what it really was, but nobody ever asks me.

The biggest dinosaur was the amphicoelias, which grew to around 58 metres long (that's more than half a football pitch!). But if you humans were around them, then you wouldn't have been too worried. Even though they would be 30 times bigger than you, they only ate vegetables, and not any meat. It would take a lot of broccoli to fill them up!

There are still dinosaurs around – up in the sky. It's almost certain that the birds you know today are direct descendants from the flying dinosaurs of millions of years ago.

You think of the dinosaur world as being a pretty dog-eat-dog place, where nothing survived long, but I'm afraid you're wrong. Fossil evidence indicates that the oldest dinosaurs actually lived to around 300 years old.

Surprisingly, four-fifths of all of the dinosaurs ever found haven't been found by the experts but by amateurs, random people like you. So if you ever have a spare few hours, get digging and see what you can find (but not in your parents' garden – they might not be too happy!)

Lively London

The world's first traffic light was installed in 1868 next to the House of Commons. It was manually operated and it didn't last too long. It blew up the next year, injuring the policeman who operated it.

More people died falling from the Monument to the Great Fire of London than died in the fire itself. The blaze destroyed enough homes to leave one out of six Londoners homeless but apparently only killed six people. In later years, seven people died from falling off the Monument before they decided putting up safety rails was a good idea.

London was the first city in the world to reach a population of 1,000,000 people, in 1811. It stayed the most populated city in the world until Tokyo overtook it in 1925.

The Houses of Parliament were built alongside the river so that when Members of Parliament passed unpopular laws a protesting mob wouldn't be able to come and surround the buildings, and the MPs could escape on boats.

London's gallows – where people were hung – was called Tyburn Tree. Around 50,000 people were hanged there over many years. Now it is a traffic island at the junction of Marble Arch and Edgware Road.

The original London Bridge was in use for around 600 years. For 355 of those years heads were stuck on spikes on it as a warning to those who thought about breaking the law.

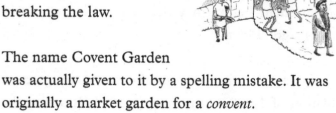

The name Covent Garden was actually given to it by a spelling mistake. It was originally a market garden for a *convent*.

Pollution used to be terrible in London. It was so bad that, in 1952, smog caused an indoors theatre performance at

Sadler's Wells to be abandoned because it was so thick that the audience couldn't see.

In 1995 a flock of small starlings landed on the minute hand of the Big Ben and they managed to delay the time it showed by five minutes.

There are dozens of lost rivers in London that used to be connected with the Thames but now they have either been built over and buried or have dried up. One of the most unusual rivers is the Westbourne. The next time you are at Sloane Square station you just need to look up to see it – it is in an overground tunnel that runs outside and above the tracks.

Tower Bridge is the iconic bridge spanning the Thames that opens to let ships go through. In 1952 it started opening as normal – except that a double decker bus was still crossing it. The driver decided that, rather than wait to be tipped over backwards as the roadway lifted, he would try to jump the (still small) gap at the midway point. The quick-thinking driver managed it, and only 12 people were injured. What was his reward for saving the lives of all of those people on board? He was given £5 and a day off work!

Foolish Phobias

The world can be a pretty scary place at times, and there's a lot of things to be afraid of. These phobias however are utterly ridiculous:

Hippopotomonstrosesquippedaliophobia – whoever named this phobia was a bit mean. This is the fear of long words!

Phobophobia is the fear of fears themselves. So if you know someone who has this, try not to remind them about it.

Didaskaleinophobia is the fear of having to go to school. Sufferers feel very anxious and sometimes are physically sick at the thought of going to school.

Dr Dino's Did You Knowbia?

When you are born you only have two fears that are built in to our DNA: everyone is afraid of loud noises and falling. It is believed that this is to help babies survive as it motivates them to alert others to danger in precarious situations. Every other fear that we have is learned during our lives.

Nomophobia is a modern problem. It's the fear of not having your phone on you, and comes from shortening 'no-mobile-phone-phobia'.

Samhainophobia is the fear of Halloween.

Anatidaephobia is probably the weirdest phobia in the world. It is the fear that somewhere in the world a duck is always watching you. People who suffer from this truly believe that they are going to be followed around by ducks wherever they go. A trip to the park is out of the question.

Dramatic Dreams

The human brain can do a lot of things, but it can't make people up. All of the strangers that you see in your dreams, you will have seen at some point in real life, even if you can't remember them.

The average person has around 2,000 dreams a year, which is about five a night. You might think that you never dream, but that isn't true – people forget between 95% and 99% of all their dreams. What it probably means is that you just have really boring dreams, because people only remember the interesting ones.

Some people are able to control the dreams that they have, like changing it from a nightmare to a good dream.

When you are having a deep dream, your body is basically paralysed. That feeling of falling and jerking awake is your body struggling to move itself again.

Dr Dino's Did You Know?

Scientists are getting closer to being able to map the images your brain creates and put them on a screen. This will be incredibly important for people who aren't able to speak, such as stroke victims or people in a coma. But it also means that sometime soon we might be able to save our dreams as a video, and even upload them onto the Internet.

Some people dream in black and white! It is almost exclusively older people who do this, and scientists believe that it is because they used to watch black and white television. People who have watched colour TV their whole lives almost never dream in black and white.

The moments just after you have woken up are the moments when you are most creative. Salvador Dali, a famous artist who used a lot of dream-like images in his paintings, would sleep in a chair next to his paints and as soon as he woke up he would start painting.

Classic Clothes

Stinging nettles have been used for clothing for as long as linen has. When the nettles are woven together they are surprisingly soft and strong.

Silk isn't grown like cotton. Believe it or not, it actually comes from worms... Silk worms make cocoons out of the very fine fabric and these are dipped in hot water and then unravelled. The silk fibres that you get from it can sometimes be a mile long!

Before the Second World War nylon was used for stockings but, during it, nylon had to be saved to be used for parachutes. Women were so used to wearing stockings, though, that they started using make-up to paint their legs and give the impression that they had stockings on!

In ancient Rome purple was so valuable that it was against the law for anyone other than the emperor to wear anything dyed purple.

In colonial times in America corsets were worn by women at all times, except for when they bathed or were pregnant. Some people never bathed... so the corsets were occasionally known to actually rot off! What's more, corsets were often so tight that they caused the wearer's internal organs to rearrange!

Wedding dresses were not often white until the 20th century. White was too hard to clean, so most of the dresses were made in dark colours.

The bikini was named after the Bikini Atoll, where the USA tested its atomic bombs. This was because the inventor, Louis Réard, believed that they were so revealing that it would create a shock as big as the atomic bomb!

In Arabic and other Eastern cultures shoes are considered dirty, because they touch the ground and the lowest part of the body. Showing the sole of your shoe to someone is offensive. Throwing your shoe at someone is the ultimate insult.

Complex Computers

We've grown so used to computers being everywhere that we forget how recent an invention they are. The first modern computer, the Z1, was built in 1936, less than 80 years ago. If you saw it now you wouldn't recognise it as a computer – it has no keyboard or screen and all of the electronics are out in the open.

In the 1950s and 1960s supercomputers were built that filled huge rooms (the largest of these, the SAGE computer in the USA, weighed more than 250 tonnes!) and were at the cutting edge of science and research. Nowadays, even our phones have a greater ability to run programs and have more memory than they did.

Dr Dino's Did You Know?

The world of computing has changed so much in the last 50 years that modern cars have more computing power than the system which guided the first Moon landing.

Bill Gates, the founder of Microsoft and one of the wealthiest people in the world, dropped out of university.

Every single minute around 10 hours' worth of video is uploaded onto YouTube. If you sat watching videos the entire day, you would only be able to see one-six-hundredth of what had been uploaded that day.

Steve Jobs and Steve Wozniak, who started Apple, weren't always rich. In fact, the first Apple computer was made from used parts which they had scrounged off of their employers for free.

The World Wide Web was invented by Tim Berners-Lee in 1990. The very first web page was a set of instructions telling people how to use the World Wide Web. It is now estimated that more than 2,000,000,000 people use the Internet.

In 1987 Apple created a video about what they thought the future would be like. It showed a futuristic digital assistant who could be used to do things like tell you what the weather is like and set up meetings or alarms. The time stamp on the video is 16 September 2011. On 4 October 2011, Apple released Siri for iPhones – so they were wrong in their prediction by less than a month!

Marvellous Music

The song 'Happy Birthday To You' is the most famous song in the world. It is owned by Warner Music and whenever it is sung in public, the singers are meant to pay a royalty fee to Warner. You won't hear it very often in films because Warner allegedly charges $10,000 for every time it is sung!

When you are listening to music your heartbeat changes to match the beat of the music you are listening to.

If you're an aspiring gardener then here's a tip for you. Flowers apparently like listening to music because they grow faster when they can hear some.

None of The Beatles were able to read music!

In 1978 Sweden's most profitable export was the band Abba. The car-maker Volvo was in second place.

The best-selling album of all time was *Thriller* by Michael Jackson which sold around 60,000,000 copies.

In 1971 Pink Floyd played an outdoor concert at the Crystal Palace Bowl. There was a lake nearby and the rock band played so loud that hundreds of fish died!

The strings of Spanish guitars were originally made from the intestines of dead sheep. They only changed to nylon during the Second World War because all of the gut strings were being used to make surgical thread. Gross!

Monaco's national orchestra is bigger than its army.

The world's fastest rapper is a man called Ricky Brown who rapped 723 syllables in 41.27 seconds in January 2005.

The best-selling musical instrument of all time is the simple harmonica.

What's Really in Food?

If you see a hair in your food, you would always pick it out. But it's the hair you can't see that you should be watching out for. L-Cysteine is added to food like bread to make it last longer and can be found in most fast foods – and it's made primarily out of human hair.

Think twice next time before you eat vanilla, strawberry or raspberry ice cream. Part of the flavour is an additive called castoreum, which comes from a beaver's bum!

It's well-known that food warehouses aren't always the cleanest places, and in the USA the FDA (Food and Drug Administration) allow what they call 'unavoidable defects' in food. We would call them rat hairs. For every 100 grams of chocolate, there is allowed to be one rodent hair.

A can of coke has nine teaspoons of sugar in it, which is actually more sugar than you are meant to have in an entire day.

Wild salmon are pink because they eat krill, but farmed salmon don't eat krill so their flesh is grey. The pink colour is added to it with a dye.

Trashy TV

The first ad was aired on 1 July 1941. It was an advert for a Bulova Watch and it lasted 20 seconds. It only cost $9. The most expensive air time now is during the Super Bowl in the USA, during which 30 seconds of ad time has sold for $5.84 million.

The largest TV in the world measures in at 201 inches – which makes it about 16 feet wide. It's so big that it can only be kept outside. Houses just aren't big enough to hold it!

The first electronic moving image was displayed in 1926 on a TV invented by John Baird. That TV only had 30 lines of graphics (now TVs have over 1,000), so it was pretty blurry. The image was of a human face, Baird's business partner Oliver Hutchison – the first TV star.

Philo Farnsworth, one of the inventors of the first TVs, wouldn't let his children watch it. He said 'There's nothing on it worthwhile, and we're not going to watch it in this household, and I don't want it in your intellectual diet.'

Most of the laughing soundtracks that you hear on TV were recorded in the 1950s. That means that the majority of the people that you hear laughing have now died. Now that's dead funny!

The average Briton watches 25 hours of TV a week. That's 1,300 hours every year, about a sixth of your entire life!

At the end of the final episode of the popular TV show *M*A*S*H* many people had been glued to the TV for the entire 2.5 hours of the show. Most of these people needed the toilet as the show finished and in New York City so many people flushed the toilet at once that it caused the plumbing systems of New York to simply shut down.

By the time the average child leaves school they will have seen 40,000 murders on TV.

Donald Duck wasn't allowed to be shown on TV in Finland – because he isn't wearing any trousers!

The longest-running primetime TV show is *The Simpsons*. It's been running for 24 years and counting.

Mel Blanc, who was the voice of Bugs Bunny, didn't like carrots.

No matter which direction Mickey Mouse is facing, his ears always point towards the front.

Movie Magic

Pumbaa was the first animal or human to fart in a Disney movie.

Animal Planet have twice made fake documentaries about mermaids being real – and both times thousands of people fell for it.

You become so excited while watching horror movies that you burn 200 calories, which is about the same as a half-hour walk.

Shrek was modelled on a real person, a French pro wrestler called Maurice Tillet. His signature move was the Bear Hug.

Shirley Henderson played Moaning Myrtle in *Harry Potter and the Goblet of Fire*. Moaning Myrtle is the ghost of a young girl, but Shirley was 40 years old!

After the Disney movie *The Princess and the Frog* came out more than 50 children were hospitalised with salmonella after kissing frogs.

It would take more than 9,000,000 balloons to lift your house off of the ground like the one in the film *Up*.

In *Terminator 2* Arnold Schwarzenegger only says 700 words, but was paid $15,000,000. That means 'Hasta la vista, baby' costs about $85,000.

The price to build the passenger liner *Titanic* was around £3,000,000. The budget for the movie *Titanic* was £125,000,000!

Bollywood, India's movie industry, makes over 800 films a year, which is twice as many as Hollywood makes.

In *The Wizard of Oz* Judy Garland's salary was $500 a week – not that much more than Toto the dog who earned $125 a week.

Quiz

1. How many atoms are there in the human body?
   A. 120; B. 7,000,000,000,000,000,000,000,000,000;
   C. 5,000,000,000,000,000; D. 4.
2. If you are from Texas, what are you allowed to do in space?
   A. Eat a Mars bar; B. Read *The Hitchhiker's Guide to the Galaxy;* C. Vote in the USA elections; D. Play Space Invaders.
3. Who was the first person to pee in his pants on the Moon?
   A. Buzz Aldrin; B. Louis Armstrong; C. Neil Armstrong; D. Buzz Lightyear.
4. What is a youf?
   A. A young person from London; B. A type of bat; C. A muffled woof; D. A vessel for transporting liquids.
5. What is the dish Escamoles, served in Mexico?

A. The feet of a yak; B. Goat's eyeballs; C. A pig's tongue; D. Giant ant's eggs.

6. What is the Australian Gympie-Gympie tree famous for?

   A. Being the largest tree in the world; B. Eating insects that land on it; C. Being bright purple; D. Having the deadliest sting in the world.

7. What is Aldgate station on the London Underground built over?

   A. A plague pit; B. An Aztec burial ground; C. A former school; D. A dragon's lair.

8. What unusual offering was paid for footballer Ion Radu?

   A. A crate of beer; B. 700 beefsteaks; C. 500 kilograms of pork; D. A flock of geese.

9. Where does silk come from?

   A. Worm's cocoons; B. On trees; C. Bees' honey; D. Spider's webs.

10. How much of the Earth is covered with water?

    A. 5%; B. 70%; C. 80%; D. 25%

11. What happened in New York at the end of the final episode of *M*A*S*H*?

    A. The whole city cheered; B. So many people put the kettle on that it caused a blackout; C. 12 people had heart attacks from the excitement;

D. So many people went to the loo that the city's plumbing broke.

12. What is blype?

A. What your fingernails are called once you chew them off; B. The technical term for snot; C. The dead skin that peels after sunburn; D. The food you spit out.

13. How old was the world's oldest goldfish when it died?

A. 28 years old; B. 132 years old; C. 65 years old; D. 43 years old.

14. What happened in Pompeii?

A. It was buried by a volcano; B. It was the first place football was played; C. The land speed record in a car was broken; D. An earthquake swallowed the entire town.

15. What did a flock of starlings do in 1995 in London?

A. Cover every inch of Trafalgar Square; B. Poo on the same person 28 times in one minute; C. Turn the Big Ben clock back by five minutes; D. Force the driver out of a London bus and drive it down the road.

16. What is the longest fence in the world?

A. The fence around the Alcatraz prison; B. My back garden fence; C. Hadrian's Fence; D. The Dingo Fence.

17. How did Clement Vallandigham die?
    A. Trying to hold his breath for too long; B. Accidentally shooting himself in court; C. Slipping on a banana skin; D. He was hit by a meteor.
18. What aren't Buddhist monks allowed to do in Tibet?
    A. Eat cereal; B. Swat a fly; C. Reincarnate after death; D. Do cartwheels after 6pm.
19. What did people originally say when answering the phone?
    A. Howdy Partner; B. Ahoy-hoy; C. Yello; D. Wazzzzuuuupppp.
20. What can't a human brain do during sleep?
    A. Make up a human face; B. Count sheep; C. Have more than one dream a night; D. Wake you up if you hear a loud noise.

Answers

1.	B	8.	C	15.	C
2.	C	9.	A	16.	D
3.	A	10.	B	17.	B
4.	C	11.	D	18.	C
5.	D	12.	C	19.	B
6.	D	13.	D	20.	A
7.	A	14.	A		